Susan,
from within
love
to reach
to touch
to dream

to know
love

Ross '96

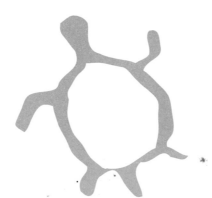

ON THE EDGE

Artistic Visions of a Shrinking Landscape

ON THE EDGE

Artistic Visions of a Shrinking Landscape

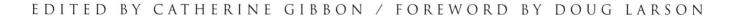

EDITED BY CATHERINE GIBBON / FOREWORD BY DOUG LARSON

THE BOSTON MILLS PRESS

CANADIAN CATALOGUING IN PUBLICATION DATA

On the edge : artistic visions of a shrinking landscape

ISBN 1-55046-153-2

1. Landscape painting, Canadian - Ontario -
Hamilton–Wentworth.   2. Hamilton–Wentworth (Ont.) -
In art.   3. Natural areas in art.   4. Painting,
Canadian - Ontario - Hamilton–Wentworth.   5. Painting,
Modern - 20th century - Ontario - Hamilton–Wentworth.
I. Gibbon, Catherine.

ND1352.C36052 1995   758'.171352'0971352
                              C95-932173-X

First published in 1995 by
The Boston Mills Press
132 Main Street
Erin, Ontario, Canada
N0B 1T0
Tel. 519 833-2407
Fax 519 833-2195

An affiliate of
Stoddart Publishing Co. Limited
34 Lesmill Road
North York, Ontario, Canada
M3B 2T6

Design by Walter J. Pick and Adele Taylor-Pick, Taylor Design Group
Printed in China

The publisher gratefully acknowledges the support of the Canada
Council, Ontario Arts Council, and Ontario Publishing Centre in the
development of writing and publishing in Canada.

Boston Mills Press books are available for bulk purchase for sales
promotions, premiums, fundraising and seminars. For details, contact:

Special Sales Department
Stoddart Publishing Co. Limited
34 Lesmill Road
North York, Ontario, Canada
M3B 2T6
Tel. 416 445-3333
Fax 416 445-5967

FOREWORD

Two decades ago, the mathematician and philosopher Jacob Bronowski presented the world with a sensitive portrayal of the development and history of human thought. By drawing on work done by hundreds of thinkers over thousands of years, Bronowski argued that the distinction between our species and others was not so much based on the presence or absence of intelligence and curiosity, but rather by our tendency to leave in our wake a vast record of that curiosity. That record—whether spoken, written, computed, drawn or sung—is our culture. It is us and it can be magnificent. Bronowski also warned, however, that people commonly and sometimes dangerously believe in cultural superiority. He argued that humans must be ever vigilant against the ascent of dogma.

In present-day Western culture the educational and legal systems are supposedly designed to prevent most forms of cultural dominance. Yet most of us are tolerant of adults who characterize young children on the basis of their artistic or scientific inclinations, and we accept fully that scientists are responsible for accurately describing the universe of facts while artists have jurisdiction over feelings.

Unfortunately, those who argue for the distinctiveness between the arts and the sciences really understand neither. Both are expressions of natural human curiosity and both represent our attempt to translate what we experience into terms that will be both understood and culturally inherited by our offspring. The scientific research that I carry out along the Niagara Escarpment, for example, will never by itself accurately describe that place. Neither will thick folios of watercolours or charcoal sketches by themselves accurately reflect the ancient cliff ecosystem of the Escarpment. But together, and especially when combined with prose, music and other forms of cultural expression, the truth of nature and humanity in this place will eventually be approached.

On the Edge represents an attempt to explore the truth about the natural environment in one place: the forests, wetlands and fields around the densely populated and heavily industrialized city of Hamilton, Ontario. The actual geographical location of the place should be immaterial to the reader. What matters is that each work presented in this volume is an accurate portrait of the real world confronting destructive forces in one place. Many of the individual pieces were conceived at exactly the same latitude and longitude, but each is unique. These differences in interpretation from observer to observer form the fluidity of culture and encourage cultural evolution. And they are as common in science as they are in the arts. What has been missing recently in Western industrialized society has been an emphasis on the interdependence of the scientific, technological, and artistic communities. Each provides to the other a sense of contrast, context, and perspective that is needed to support social policies regarding local habitat use and abuse.

On the Edge celebrates what remains and mourns what is lost. It honours whole living landscapes and fragments of beings long dead. It condemns where appropriate. It displays the joy of colour in forests free from disturbance, but also acknowledges the greyness of habitats on death row. Taken as a whole, this book is part of a growing cultural awareness of the value of intact places that can nurture us physically and spiritually. If this awareness is welded with works of science and technology that try to achieve the same goal, the combined product can form the foundation for a new sense of place. Once places around the globe are similarly treated, the sustainability of the entire planet will be assured.

Our ability to wrest the controls from those who would sacrifice the earth for their immediate gratification is dependent on us hearing and acting on the message of *On the Edge*. Listen.

Doug Larson

Doug Larson is a scientist and environmentalist whose innovative approach to scientific research has led to discoveries of global importance by simply taking a close look at what goes on around us in our near natural environment. Currently teaching at the University of Guelph, Larson is best known as the individual who discovered the ancient trees growing on the Niagara Escarpment.

PREFACE

Close proximity to a natural environment—being in nature—alters all of us in ways which remain pretty much unexplored, even undescribed, in our culture.

Sharon Butala

The Head of the Lake, or Hamilton–Wentworth, as it is known to its present inhabitants, is a place of edges. Defined by the shores of Lake Ontario and the encircling arm of the Niagara Escarpment, its marshes, cliffs, and protected valleys provide habitats that sustain numerous and diverse forms of life. For ten thousand years, generations of native people co-existed here with a primeval forest environment whose fertility and vigour defy our imagination. To the indigenous people, this landscape was resonant with spirituality. Their reverence for the land is expressed in their myths and oral traditions, some of which portray the Niagara Escarpment as a sacred place.

Two hundred years ago, Western culture began to exert its influence on this landscape without the guidance of an indigenous sense of place. Consequently, our relationship with the natural landscape needs to be continually renewed. We call this a new land, but it is really very ancient. What is new is the way we think about it. And the way we think about it is evident in the manner in which we have altered the landscape at the Head of the Lake in the last two hundred years. It is as occupants rather than custodians of this land that we have pushed our natural environment toward the edge of its capacity to create and nurture life. For without an inner understanding of the place we inhabit, we have neither the means nor the need to conserve it.

And so, the concept for this book was born in a time and place of edges.

The idea of using art to promote environmental awareness is not a new one. In Temagami, Ontario, and the Carmanah Valley, British Columbia, precedents of the ON THE EDGE project have successfully drawn attention to the destruction of these wilderness areas. Central to these projects and to ON THE EDGE is the belief that art can effect positive environmental change through the power of its imagery. But ON THE EDGE begins where these projects left off. Using a local context to explore the universal themes of attachment to landscape, it is less about a place than about a sense of place.

The development of a sense of place is an ongoing process. Like genetic material, it is passed on from generation to generation, and like the layers of limestone that make up the edge of the Niagara Escarpment, each encounter with the land adds another layer of depth. It requires more than an experience of sight, sound, and smell. It is an inward journey of connections: between people and place, and between past and present. As Barry Lopez says, it is precisely what is invisible in the landscape that makes it important. *On the Edge: Artistic Visions of a Shrinking Landscape* strives to make the invisible visible.

The material presented in this book moves thematically from the generalities of "Sense of Place" to the specifics in "Spirits of Place." "Simple Gifts" presents some of the benefits derived from natural areas. In the chapters "The Shrinking Landscape" and "Renewal," both the abuse of our environment and solutions for improvement are explored.

The quotations are drawn from many sources: historical and contemporary, local and universal. Their greatest rewards can be appreciated through repeated readings and even commitment to memory, where they can be re-evaluated in the context of one's own personal experience. All of the images in this book were produced by artists interpreting their own bioregion under the auspices of the ON THE EDGE Art/Environment project. As such, they interpret a variety of threatened ecosystems within the Niagara Escarpment region's Carolinian forest. Many of the works of art were inspired by direct experience in three distinctive natural areas where the artists' camps took place: the Beverly Swamp, the Dundas Valley, and the Red Hill Valley. The depth of these encounters is shown in the humour, imagination and poetry of these images. Their power resides in their ability to define and convey an inner experience of place.

In one sense, this book documents individual intuitive encounters with place by the people who share a relationship with it. In another, it is a map of our collective consciousness, furthering our understanding of what is particular, unique and intimate about where we live. In *On the Edge*, the near landscape is seen as the point of reference that shapes our visions. It is its very nearness that makes it important. Through these artistic visions we move from depiction of place to definition of place, from detail to abstraction, and from occupants to custodians of the land. For until we experience landscape as a state of mind rather than a capital resource, we will continue to be *On the Edge* of destroying the exuberant creativity inherent in the natural world.

Catherine Gibbon

SENSE OF PLACE

It is only in a country that is well-known, full of

familiar names and places, full of life that is always

changing, that the mind goes free of abstractions,

and renews itself in the presence of the creation,

that so persistently eludes human comprehension

and human law. It is only in the place that one

belongs to, intimate and familiar, long watched

over, that the details rise up out of the whole and

become visible...

Wendell Berry
Recollected Essays

Linda Hankin, *By the Barn Overlooking the Valley*, oil on canvas, 64x52 cm, 1992.

Until we understand what the land is, we are at odds with everything we touch. And to come to that understanding it is necessary, even now, to leave the regions of our conquest—the cleared fields, the towns and cities, the highways—and re-enter the woods. For only there can a man encounter the silence and the darkness of his own absence. Only in this silence and darkness can he recover the sense of the world's longevity, of its ability to thrive without him, of his inferiority to it and his dependence on it. Perhaps then, having heard that silence and seen that darkness, he will grow humble before the place and begin to take it in—to learn *from it* what it is. As its sounds come into his hearing, and its lights and colours come into his vision, and its odors come into his nostrils, then he may come into *its* presence as he never has before, and he will arrive in his place and will want to remain. His life will grow out of the ground like the other lives of the place, and take its place among them. He will be *with* them—neither ignorant of them, nor indifferent to them, nor against them— and so at last he will grow to be native-born.

That is, he must re-enter the silence and the darkness, and be born again.

Wendell Berry
Recollected Essays

PATRICIA KOZOWYK, *Winter Woods*, CHALK PASTEL ON PAPER, 71x100 CM, 1993.

No, the human heart

Is unknowable.

But in my birthplace

The flowers still smell

The same as always.

Tsurayaki (AD 882–946)
One Hundred Poems from the Japanese

LINDA HANKIN, *Wildflowers*, OIL ON LINEN, 33x34.5 CM, 1993.

I think of two landscapes—one outside the self, the other within. The external landscape is the one we see—not only the line and colour of the land and its shading at different times of the day, but also its plants and animals in season, its weather, its geology, the record of its climate and evolution...

What makes the landscape comprehensible are the relationships between them. One learns a landscape finally not by knowing the name or identity of everything in it, but by perceiving the relationships in it—like that between the sparrow and the twig...

The second landscape I think of is an interior one, a kind of projection within a person of a part of the exterior landscape.... Similarly, the speculations, intuitions, and formal ideas we refer to as "mind" are a set of relationships in the interior landscape with purpose and order; some of these are obvious, many impenetrably subtle. The shape and character of these relationships in a person's thinking, I believe, are deeply influenced by where on this earth one goes, what one touches, the patterns one observes in nature—the intricate history of one's life in the land, even a life in the city, where wind, the chirp of birds, the line of a falling leaf, are known...the interior landscape responds to the character and subtlety of an exterior landscape; the shape of the individual mind is affected by land as it is by genes.

Barry Lopez
Crossing Open Ground

OWEN FORD, *Untitled*, OIL ON MASONITE, 50x60 CM, 1991.

It is precisely what is *invisible* in the land that makes what is merely empty space to one person a *place* to another. The feeling that a particular place is suffused with memories, the specific focus of sacred and profane stories, and that the whole landscape is a congeries of such places, is what is meant by a local sense of the land...

The differing landscapes of the earth are hard to know individually. They are as difficult to engage in conversation as wild animals. The complex feelings of affinity and self assurance one feels with one's native place rarely develop again in another landscape...

It is easy to underestimate the power of a long-term association with the land, not just with a specific spot but with the span of it in memory and imagination, how it fills, for example, one's dreams. For some people, what they are is not finished at the skin, but continues with the reach of the senses out into the land. If the land is summarily disfigured or reorganized, it causes them psychological pain. Again, such people are attached to the land as if by luminous fibers; and they live in a kind of time that is not of the moment but, in concert with memory, extensive, measured by a lifetime. To cut these fibers causes not only pain but a sense of dislocation.

Barry Lopez
Arctic Dreams

JOHN DAVIES, *Escarpment Forest*, OIL ON CANVAS, 92x122 CM, 1993.

The shining water that moves in the streams and

rivers is not just water but the blood of our ancestors.

If we sell you our land, you must remember that it is

sacred and that each ghostly reflection in the clear

water of the lakes tells of events and memories in the

life of my people. The water's murmur is the voice of

my father's father.

*One of several versions of Chief Seattle's speech
delivered in 1854 in response to the U.S. government's
purchase offer for his tribal lands.*

LYNN MACINTYRE, *Swamp Maze* (detail from composite photographic print), SILVER GELATIN PRINT, 28x96.5 CM, 1992.

In 1785, William Cope, his wife, aged mother-in-law, and five sons, with their wives and children, left their comfortable homes in New York State and started for Upper Canada. There they intended to make a home in the wilderness, in a land where the Union Jack could still wave. Carrying their household goods with them they travelled many weary miles...and made their way by boat along the shores of the lake to Burlington Bay.

The small boats were heavily laden and several times they were swamped and their occupants soaked in the icy water. So they would be forced to land and build great fires to dry their clothing and warm their chilled limbs. The old grandmother was their greatest care. Often the sturdy grandsons would carry her from the boat to be the first on the beach, for she, brave woman, was a hundred years old, and she had come with them to end her days in the wilderness.

They landed at the place where Hamilton now stands, a swampy district overgrown with Indian grass. The mosquitoes and rattlesnakes drove them farther inland.... It was April when they came and started pioneer life in that dense forest.

With only axe and auger for tools, they built their log cabin, using clay for plaster, and basswood bark for roofing. They cleared a little field and planted Indian corn. Apple seeds, too, were planted, that later grew into fruitful trees, and a little garden flourished in the heart of the forest.

The aged grandmother lived for seven years in that new home. She loved to wander through the little garden and watch the green things grow. In the late summer days it was her delight to pick the green cucumbers that grew so well in that rich soil. The spicy breath from the pines would fan her wrinkled cheek as she stood there thinking of her childhood's home. Did her dim old eyes see the lovely panorama that stretched before her - the hills and valleys, the forest, and beyond, the glint of that blue inland sea? At the ripe age of one hundred and seven she was "gathered unto her fathers," the first white woman laid to rest in the wilderness of Beverly pines.

Reminiscences of eighty-six-year-old Mrs. Inksetter (great-granddaughter of William Cope and great-grandmother of David Inksetter, the present owner of Inksetter apple farm, near Dundas, Ontario), 1916.
"Papers and Records of the Wentworth Historical Society"

MARY MCGINN, *View from Inksetter Farm*, CHALK PASTEL ON PAPER, 54x74 CM, 1992.

FURTHER ARRIVALS

After we had crossed the long illness
that was the ocean, we sailed up-river

On the first island
the immigrants threw off their clothes
and danced like sandflies

We left behind one by one
the cities rotting with cholera,
one by one our civilized
distinctions

and entered a large darkness.

It was our own
ignorance we entered.

I have not come out yet

My brain gropes nervous
tentacles in the night, sends out
fears hairy as bears,
demands lamps; or waiting

for my shadowy husband, hears
malice in the trees' whispers.

I need wolf's eyes to see
the truth.

I refuse to look in a mirror.

Whether the wilderness is
real or not
depends on who lives there.

Margaret Atwood
The Journals of Susanna Moodie

AUDREY SHIMIZU, *New Growth*, CONTE AND PENCIL, 60x45 CM, 1991.

Everything is tied with nature. The land, rocks, trees

are part of our history, a part of us. They live longer

than we do. If you stay in one place, a tree will watch

you crawl, run, walk, shuffle, and eventually see your

children complete the cycle behind you.

Ruby Slipperjack
"Interview." Contemporary Challenges:
Conversations with Native Writers

SPIRITS OF PLACE

In the forest think of the forest,

not of this tree and that

but the singing movement of the whole.

Emily Carr
Hundreds and Thousands: Journals of an Artist

Gillian Quick, *Dream Valley,* chalk pastel on paper, 50x65 cm, 1993.

Page 30

NAKED TREES

Naked trees extend their complicated praise
branches sway, in
    a sort of unison
not agreed upon
    each their own way
to the one wind
    die down, as the wind dies
Dendritic limbs converge
    chute to common ground
column down to earth
    It is this trunk
which stands between its own two extremes
Out of sight
    roots are gripped in unanimity
break surface with a singleness of mind, which
ten feet up
    begins to subdivide

John Terpstra
Naked Trees

Patricia Kozowyk, *Maple,* chalk pastel on paper, 91.5x112 cm, 1991.

Page 32

BRANCHES

Trees are intended to move. Although
rooted to one spot, trees are expected to be
in some kind of constant motion. No tree is ever entirely still.
The movement of growth is indiscernible, but indisputable: a
given. And the delectable shifting of branch and leaf, the
minute swaying of the trunk!

A tree moves because it must. The wind blows and it cannot refuse.

It moves toward nothing, but flails the same bit of air.

The youngest branches—those furthest up—tend to be the
wild ones, and become at times unruly. The older, middle
branches are by now less easily influenced and provide a
much-needed steadying effect. While the trunk itself moves
only in the most dire circumstance.

Yet just beneath the trunk's sombre, unyielding exterior
flows a liquid concentrate, and it is this wondrous substance which,
when it has coursed much diluted into those upper
reaches, becomes the cause of their remarked frenzy.

The tree, in effect, filling its own sails; creator of wind, and of the
seeming stillness.

John Terpstra
Naked Trees

BARRY HODGSON, *Beech, Dundas,* OIL ON CANVAS, 61x51 CM, 1991.

Page 34

ADOLESCENCE

A sapling is no more than a tapered tube, a two-by-two. Six feet up
from the ground it projects awkward looking sticks left and right
that end in bursts of leaf, bigger than expected. The leaves
themselves oversized, out of proportion to the skinny branch.

Incongruities. The forms of adolescence.

When it bends in the wind, it bends beyond the point you'd intu-
itively feel has no return. What business has wood being so pliant?

However, elastic as it is, and because it must, the sapling pretends to
the tree it envisions. There is no turning back to the seed. Once it
has raised its head above the undergrowth it mimics the eventual
outcome, behaves as if the goal were already reached, as if its future
were fully contained within it now: home for the wildlife, shade of
the nations below. The absurdity of this is transparent of course, as
obvious to the eye as the ultimate fragility of the stick figure itself.

Then, again, the wind blows.

John Terpstra
Naked Trees

MICHAEL DOBSON, *Saturday Afternoon, Dundas Valley,* WATERCOLOUR, 56x76 CM, 1991.

Page 36

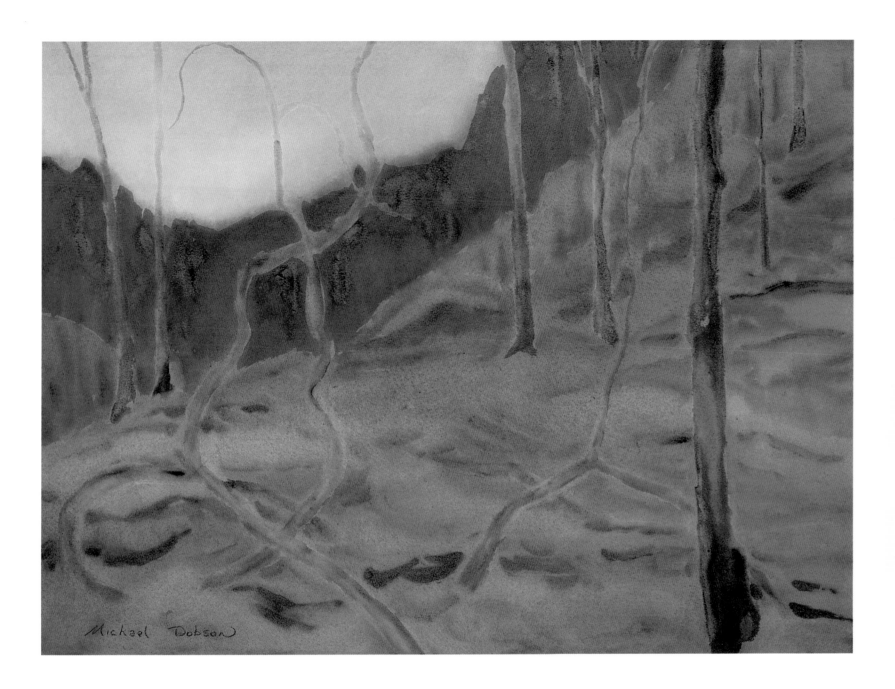
Michael Dobson

ASPENS

A sweet high treble threads its silvery song,

Voice of the restless aspen, fine and thin

It trills its pure soprano, light and long—

Like the vibrato of a mandolin.

Tekahionwake (Pauline Johnson)
Flint and Feather

Catherine Gibbon, *Silver Light,* chalk pastel on paper, 81x102 cm, 1992.

Page 38

Mr. Hatch wrote acknowledging the two paper sketches

I sent him. He found their vigour and profoundness

appealing. Said few people understand them. Now I

can't see what there is to be understood. They are just

woodsy statements, no secrets or obscurities beyond the

fact that all life is a mystery. Perhaps folk would like a

numbered bit on the back: 1. a tree 2. a root 3. a grass

4. a fool looking. Oh life, life, how queer you are!

Emily Carr
Hundreds and Thousands: Journals of an Artist

BETTY SWANWICK, *Tree Song,* ACRYLIC ON CANVAS, 82x112 CM, 1993.

Page 40

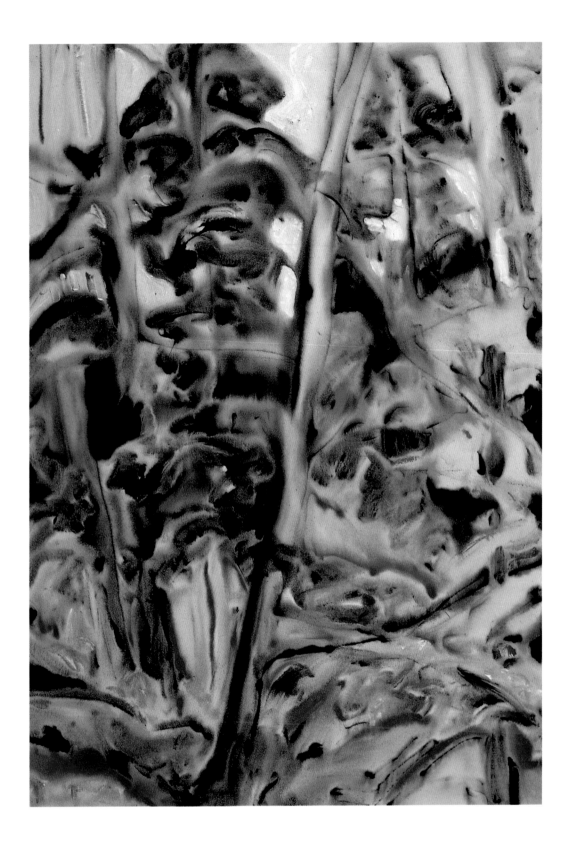

FROM THE MOST DISTANT TIME

Majestic, from the most distant time,

The sun rises and sets.

Time passes and men cannot stop it.

The four seasons serve them,

But do not belong to them.

The years flow like water.

Everything passes away before my eyes.

The Emperor Wu of Han (AD 156–187)
Love and the Turning Year;
One Hundred Poems from the Chinese

SIMPLE GIFTS

The great sea has set me in motion.

Set me adrift,

And I move as a weed in the river.

The arch of sky

And mightiness of storms

Encompasses me,

And I am left

Trembling with joy.

Inuit Song

CATHERINE GIBBON, *Thunderbolt,* CHALK PASTEL ON PAPER, 100x150 CM, 1994.

Page 46

Very early in the morning of today, I did get out of my bed and I did get dressed in a quick way. Then I climbed out the window of the house we live in. The sun was up, and the birds were singing. I went my way. As I did go, I did have hearing of many voices—they were the voices of earth, glad for the spring. They did say what they had to say in the growing grass, and in the leaves growing out from tips of branches. The birds did have knowing, and sang what the grasses and leaves did say of the gladness of living. I too did feel glad feels, from my toes to my curls.

I went down by the swamp. I went there to get reeds. There I saw a black bird with red upon his wings. He was going in among the rushes. I made a stop to watch him. I have thinks tomorrow I must be going in among the rushes, where he did go. I shall pull off my shoes and stockings first, for mud is there, and there is water. I like to go in among the rushes where the black birds with red upon their wings do go. I like to touch fingertips with the rushes. I like to listen to the voices that whisper in the swamp. And I do so like to feel the mud ooze up between my toes. Mud has so much of interest in it—slippery feels, and sometimes little seeds that some-day will grow into plant-folk, if they do get the right chance. And some were so growing this morning, and more were making begins—I did have seeing of them while I was looking looks about for reeds.

With the reeds I did find there, I did go a-piping. I went adown the creek, and out across the field, and in along the lane. Every stump I did come to, I did climb upon...

Most every day, I do dance. I dance with the leaves and the grass. I feel thrills from my toes to my curls. I feel like a bird, sometimes. Then I spread my arms for wings, and I go my way from stump to stump, and on adown the hill. Sometimes I am a demoiselle, flitting near unto the water. Then I nod unto the willows, and they nod unto me. They wave their arms, and I wave mine. They wiggle their toes in the water a bit, and I do so, too. And every time we wiggle our toes, we do drink into our souls the song of the brook—the glad song it is always singing. And the joy-song does sing on in our hearts. So it did today.

> Opal Whiteley (excerpt from a diary written between the ages of six and nine)
> *The Singing Creek Where the Willows Grow; the Rediscovered Diary of Opal Whiteley*

ANONYMOUS, FROM THE COLLECTION OF THE HAMILTON BOARD OF EDUCATION (SEE COPYRIGHT ACKNOWLEDGEMENTS), TEMPERA ON PAPER, 45x60 CM,

The birch tree suffered enormously from the itch, he squirmed; he writhed in discomfort. Though he had numerous limbs, arms, and fingers, he could not scratch. There was nothing the birch tree could do to relieve his sufferings.

In his agony the poor birch called out to the squirrels and porcupines and beavers to pick out the ticks, grubs, and beetles that were tormenting him. But the squirrels and porcupines and beavers were too busy to offer any help. The best they could do was to give their sympathy without limit.

Next the birch called out to the birds. They too felt sorry for the birch, but they could do nothing. Only the woodpeckers came to help. Coming to the aid of the poor tree the downy woodpecker, his cousin, the red-headed woodpecker, the flicker, and the chickadee all picked every pest from beneath the bark of the birch. The birch tree ceased itching.

Many years later the woodpeckers were in distress. Not knowing what to do or from whom they could find help, they, at last came to the birch and related a sad story. In the long rain-less spell, the woodpeckers were dying from thirst. The woodpeckers were unable to drink from pools and lakes and streams like other birds could.

"Could," they asked, "you do something?"

The birch remembering the help that he had received from the woodpeckers said to them, "Go to my trunk and drill two holes near each other and they will presently fill up with my sap."

The desperate woodpeckers flew down and drummed away at the trunk of the tree, until they had drilled two tiny holes. Almost immediately the holes began to fill up and yield a rich flow of sap. Thirstily, the woodpeckers drank and they have been drinking from trees since that time.

Basil Johnston
Ojibway Heritage

ELIZABETH HALLIWELL, *Trees Please,* WATERCOLOUR ON PAPER, 51x33 CM, 1993.

Why is running water such balm to the human spirit? Why do we sleep more soundly beside a waterfall than in the quiet forest? Better even than the rainbow, I think, it represents for us the continuing process of life on our planet. The flow of water is the cycle of fertility renewing itself; it happens only because the sun has been shining, the mists rising, and the rains falling in the distant hills. A deep human instinct of involvement in the onward flow of life, of the cyclical movements of nature, has given us this archetype of flowing water, the sound of it telling us that the world is alive, like the sound of a heart beating beside us in sleep.

Harold Horwood
Dancing on the Shore

PATRICK BERMINGHAM, *Red Hill Creek*, OIL ON PAPER, 41x51 CM, 1992.

THE PEACE OF WILD THINGS

When despair for the world grows in me
and I wake in the night at the least sound
in fear of what my life and my children's lives may be,
I go and lie down where the wood drake
rests in his beauty on the water, and the great heron feeds.
I come into the peace of wild things
who do not tax their lives with forethought
of grief. I come into the presence of still water.
And I feel above me the day-blind stars
waiting with their light. For a time
I rest in the grace of the world, and am free.

Wendell Berry
Collected Poems

The most exemplary nature is that of the topsoil.
It is very Christ-like in its passivity and beneficence,
and in the penetrating energy that issues out of
its peaceableness. It increases by experience, by
the passage of seasons over it, growth rising out
of it and returning to it, not by ambition or
aggressiveness. It is enriched by all things that die
and enter into it. It keeps the past, not as
history or as memory, but as richness, new
possibility. Its fertility is always building up out
of death into promise. Death is the bridge or the
tunnel by which its past enters its future.

Wendell Berry
Recollected Essays

NANCY HUNTER, *Nature's Cycle,* OIL ON MYLAR, 60x38 CM, 1991.

Matter is forever being ground down into amorphous dust and earth, and is forever rebuilding itself into the beautiful lattices of crystalline order, denying, even before life appears, that the universe is decaying into a heat sink or collapsing into a black hole. Rather, the principles of organization, of complex geometrical harmony, of all the forms of symmetry, are inherent in the most primitive levels of chemical evolution, and are certainly as much a part of the basic stuff of our universe as are the particles and waves and electro-magnetic fields that underlie every thing we see and know and apprehend.

Harold Horwood
Dancing on the Shore

Doug Moore, *Trees Round Pond,* oil on wood, 41x53 cm, 1991.

Rhythm begins far down in nature, perhaps as far down as the resonance of fundamental particles—which may, after all, be not quite so fundamental as once was supposed; it paces the universal dance of the molecules; it is inherent in the quartz crystals that keep our watches running on time. The earth dances with the sun and the moon, creating the regular rhythm of day and night, of summer and winter, of spring tide and neap tide. All those rhythms in turn are transmitted to living creatures: we see them most notably in the slow dance of the sea anemones in the tidal pool, in the rising and falling of the worms on a clam flat. Even in the darkness of a laboratory tank, shut away from the daylight and the outside world, such creatures will continue the rhythms that their ancestors learned on the shores of some vanished ocean, taught to them by the dance of the solar system, in the years when life was young

Order, pattern, symmetry, rhythm—all may seem to be abstract qualities, not to be considered in a class with matter and energy. And yet, when we think about the question, we may conclude that these abstract qualities could be just as fundamental to the universe as the "forces" that bind the elemental particles into atoms.... Order, pattern, symmetry, and rhythm operate at the highest and lowest levels of perception.

Harold Horwood
Dancing on the Shore

Barbara Guy-Long, *Dancing on the Edge,* acrylic on paper, 65x101.75 cm, 1992.

A Lesson from the Teaching Garden

The bay is called Cootes Paradise, after
a man named Cootes. The path out to its verge
that loses the last, grey, staggered roof-tops
with a casual turn, does not fold back

until across the break it stands in clear
prospect of Arcadia. Below the hills
I can make out the thumb of a small lake
that presses (it must seem from high above)

into the soft dough of the wood, rising
on three sides around it, lightly crusted
and browned by the November fallen leaves.

The pond-drink gathers debris like tea-bract
at the brim, glinting ciphers from the stirred
duff and sediment that I have come to read.

But that isn't what I see. The night frost
has left in the inlet a thin clear patina,
an ice-skin that puckers on the water
where a small finch goes out to leave his prints.

The light strengthens. For a little while
that sheen over the bay's black element
will brace the morning's flurry where it fell,
rose winded, and fell again like cold down.

And it will not give, look long as I wish,
not now, and not when the ice it rests on
darkens to water. If I came for more

than the brief levity where no sound
nor any brighter spectacle will keep me
from going unchanged, it would be all the same.

Jeffery Donaldson

E. Robert Ross, *Cootes Paradise*, acrylic on hardboard, 91.5x112 cm, 1995.

Page 62

THE SHRINKING LANDSCAPE

Now that we have changed the most basic forces around us, the noise of that chain saw will always be in the woods. We have changed the atmosphere, and that will change the weather. The temperature and rainfall are no longer to be entirely the work of some separate, uncivilizable force, but instead in part a product of our habits, our economies, our ways of life. Even in the most remote wilderness, where the strictest laws forbid the felling of a single tree, the sound of that saw will be clear, and a walk in the woods will be changed- tainted by its whine. The world outdoors will mean much the same thing as the world indoors, the hill the same thing as the house...

We have built a greenhouse, a human creation, where once there bloomed a sweet and wild garden.

Bill McKibben
The End of Nature

"Conservation"

Beaudette '92

THE TREES WILL DIE

An increase of one degree in average temperature
moves the climatic zones thirty-five to fifty miles
north.... The trees will die. Consider nothing more
than that—just that the trees will die.
                    Bill McKibben, *The End of Nature*

Late in Vermont let me consider
some familiar trees I've lived among
    for thirty years of sleet and snow,
        of sun and rain: The aspens
quaking silver when the wet winds blow;

    the white oaks, with their seven-lobed leaves
        and gently furrowed bark,
whose April buds sprout reddish-brown;
        and I'll consider pin oaks
    their stiff branches sloping down

asserting their own space, and sculpted leaves,
    flaming vermilion in the fall,
holding on, even when they're curled and dry,
        through freezing winter storms
    which keep us huddled, you and I,

around a fire that woos us back to feel
        what our ancestors felt
    some sixty thousand years ago;
and I'll consider red oaks with their pointy leaves,
    shiny dark trunks that seem to know

        the secret of slow growth,
    a message safe to pass along.
And then, considering the plenitude
    of maples here, I'll start with sugar
for its syrup and its symmetry, its brood

    of tiny yellow flower clusters
in the spring, and in the autumn such a blaze
        of orange, gold, and red,

whatever gloom might form the drizzling weather
    in my doom-reflecting head,

relief comes from the self-forgetfulness
        of looking at what's there-
    the trees, the multitude of trees.
I stop here to consider in the brief years left
        to praise them and to please

    you who have loved their scented shade,
their oceanic choiring in the wind. And so I'll list
        a few more that I know:
    the silver maple and the willow and the birch,
        box elder, basswood, and the shadblow

        whose pinkish-white flowers
    quicken the awakened woods
and quicken me. And then the spruce and pines,
        their slender, tapered cones,
        glimmering intricate designs

that tempt astonished eyes to contemplate
        how and indifferent force—
    just evolutionary randomness,
        yet so like old divinity—
    could wrest such pattern from initial emptiness.

    Before our history began
        the void commanded
there be congregated trees and creatures filled
        with words to mimic them
        and represent the moods that spilled

out of the creatures' thoughts into the world,
    so that the trees and names for trees
        would then be joined as one:
    the melancholy hemlocks in the humming dark,
        the tamaracks which flare gold in the sun

        as if to hold the light
of wavering October in their arms
        a little longer, as I do—
yet though they're evergreens at heart,
        like me, my dear, and you,

they lose their needles when the cold comes on.
    And as the tilted planet turns
to offer us fresh colours that embellish speech,
        more names rush into view:
the sycamore, the cedar, and the beech,

        horse-chestnut, butternut,
the hickories, black walnut, and of course
        the cornucopia of fruits—
apple and cherry, pear and plum and peach,
        each with a tang that suits

        the palate of whatever taste
one might have dreamed of ripened paradise.
        When I consider how
a man-made shift in climate of a few degrees
        reveals the rebel power we now

        have learned to cultivate
in order to subdue the animals
        and take dominion, like a curse,
over the fields, the forests, and the atmosphere—
        as if the universe

        belonged to us alone—I wonder
if consideration of the family of trees
        might give us pause
and let us once again obey the sun,
        whose light commands all human laws.

                    Robert Pack

Juliet Jancso, *Encroachment*, ceramic, lead and cloth, 71x92x74 cm, 1993.

I am Haunani-Kay Trask, a descendant of the Pi'ilani line of Maui and the Kahakumakaliua line of Kaua'i. I greet you as an indigenous woman. As indigenous peoples, our nationalism is born not of predatory consumption... but of genealogical connection to our place....

This indigenous knowledge is not unique to Hawaiians, but it is shared by most indigenous peoples throughout the world....We are stewards of the Earth, our mother, and we offer an ancient, umbilical wisdom about how to protect and ensure her life.

The lessons of our cultures have never been more crucial to global survival.... No one knows how better to care for Hawai'i, our island home, than those of us who have lived here for thousands of years. On the other side of the world from us, no people understand the desert better than those who inhabit her. And so on, throughout the magnificently varied places of the Earth. Forest people know the forests; mountain people know the mountains; plains people know the plains.

...If this is our heritage, then the counter to the New World Order is not more uniformity or more conformity, but more autonomy, more localized control of resources and the cultures they can maintain. Human diversity *ensures* biodiversity....The more we are made to be the same, the more the environment we inhabit becomes the same.

As the people are transformed, or more likely, exterminated, their environment is progressively degraded...Physical despoliation is reflected in cultural degradation. A dead land is preceded by a dying people. As an example, indigenous languages replaced by "universal" (read "colonial") languages result in the creation of "dead languages." But what is "dead" or "lost" is not the language but the people who once spoke it and transmitted their mother tongue to succeeding generations. Lost, too, is the relationship between words and their physical referents. Here, in Hawai'i, English is the major language, but it cannot begin to feel the physical beauty of our islands in the unparalleled detail of the Hawaiian language. Nor can English reveal how we knew animals to be our family; how we harnessed the ocean's rhythms...nor how we sailed from hemisphere to hemisphere with nothing but the stars to guide us.

The secrets of the land die with the people of the land. This is the bitter lesson of the modern age.

Haunani-Kay Trask
Malama 'Aina: Take Care of the Land

Tracey Bowen, *Swamp Angel*, mixed media with wood, metal and coloured xerox, 40x23x10 cm, 1992.

We abuse land because we regard it as a commodity belonging to us. When we see land as a community to which we belong, we may begin to use it with love and respect. There is no other way for land to survive the impact of mechanized man, nor for us to reap from it the esthetic harvest it is capable, under science, of contributing to culture.

That land is a community is the basic concept of ecology, but that land is to be loved and respected is an extension of ethics.

Aldo Leopold
A Sand County Almanac

GORD PULLAR, *Buttermilk Falls,* ACRYLIC, INK, AND PASTEL, 122x151 CM, 1992.

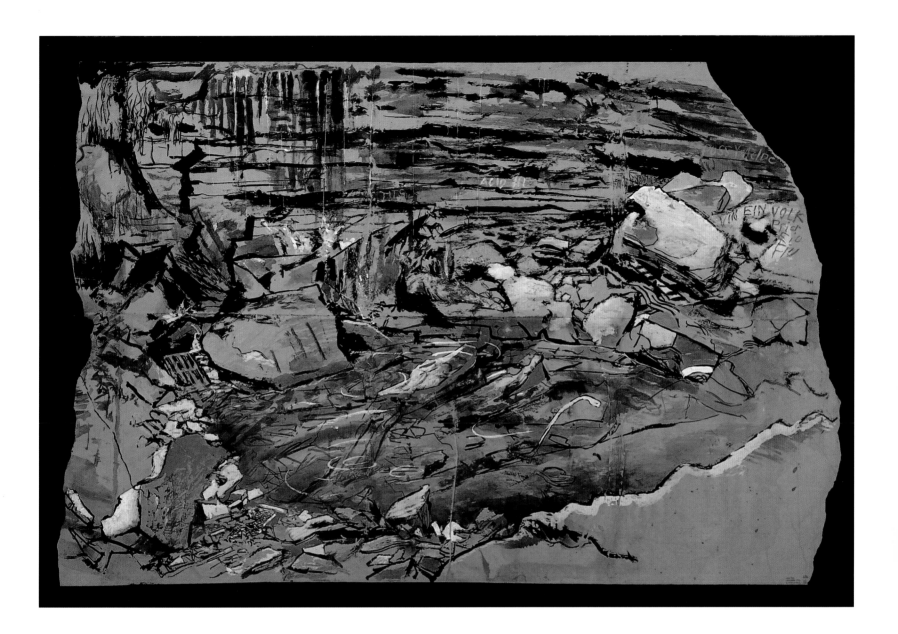

PASSENGER PIGEONS

About 1860, residents of this region frequently saw vast flocks of Passenger or Wood pigeons, millions in numbers, flying from dawn until dusk, east to west, over that area between Mount Albion and the Red Hill, at a height of about four hundred feet. At the corner of the mountain above Bartonville, many of them were struck down with sticks, and used for food. Forty years later, not one of these pigeons could be found in America, although a reward of one thousand dollars was offered for a single specimen. Their complete extinction is one of the mysteries of natural history on this continent.

J.E. Turner
The History of Albion Mills (1946)

JANICE KOVAR, *Crow Song,* ACRYLIC ON PANEL, 122x163 CM, 1993.

...we have assumed that our lives need have no real connection to the natural world, that our minds are separate from our bodies, and that as disembodied intellects we can manipulate the world in any way we choose. Precisely because we feel no connection to the physical world, we trivialize the consequences of our actions. And because this linkage seems abstract, we are slow to understand what it means to destroy those parts of the environment that are crucial to our survival. We are, in effect, bulldozing the Gardens of Eden.

Al Gore
Earth in the Balance

BOB BARKWELL, *Load Lifter 2200*, SILVER GELATIN PHOTOGRAPHIC PRINT, 28x35 CM, 1991.

Page 76

If I were an alien from outer space I would see the map of this forest as a single live fabric...
The forest grows like a complex membrane at the interface of solid rock and gaseous
atmosphere, drawing from and contributing to both. Only when one gets close to it,
armed with a field guide, perhaps, can one pick out each biological stitch and give it a
name, a spurious separateness, which—in its intricately threaded life—it doesn't have
and never has had. The fabric can be raveled, worn, made dull.... We can crush, snip,
and wear it away.

I find all this very impressive. We can crush and snip and get away with it. Why not?
It's fun, it has its advantages. The fabric slips a knot here and there with every species
pushed to extinction, every ton of hydrogen sulphide pumped into the air, every acre
paved. I wonder if this isn't a form of jolly suicide. Won't our supporting fabric collapse
under our weight if we keep this up? Well, yes. Everyone knows this. But it isn't a subject that one mentions in polite company, just as one doesn't graphically describe a
degenerative disease.... The avoidance seems to make the problem of our use of power
even more visible.... By avoiding I cut myself off. Most of the time I manage to see
these hills as a fabric I can bounce on, that I am free to tamper with, even smash and
stain at will like a spoiled and unloved child. This avoidance of the issue can be wonder-
fully subtle; for instance, you cannot, after all, lightheartedly bulldoze a friend. So it is
convenient to make of trees things that are no longer our friends but manipulable objects.
I was convinced, for a long time, that trees were not really alive; not *really alive*.
Sometimes I still manage to convince myself of this, but it is not as easy.

Diana Kappel-Smith
Wintering

JIM RILEY, *Red Hill Valley Under Pressure* (detail), PHOTO MANIPULATION, 12x17 CM, 1993.

Something will have gone out of us as a people if
we ever let the remaining wilderness be destroyed;
if we permit the last virgin forests to be turned
into comic books and plastic cigarette cases; if we
drive the few remaining members of the wild
species into zoos or to extinction; if we pollute the
last clear air and dirty the last clean streams and
push our paved roads through the last of the
silence, so that never again will people be free in
their own country from the noise, the exhausts,
the stinks of human and automotive waste. And
so that never again can we have the chance to see
ourselves single, separate, vertical and individual in
the world, part of the environment of trees and
rocks and soil, brother to the other animals, part of
the natural world and competent to belong in it.
Without any remaining wilderness we are commit-
ted wholly, without chance for even momentary
reflection and rest, to a headlong drive into our
technological termite-life, the Brave New World of
a completely man-controlled environment.

Wallace Stegner
The Sound of Mountain Water

ROBERT CLARK YATES, *Red Hill Valley,* ACRYLIC ON CANVAS, 145x71 CM, 1993.

The difference between a path and a road is not only the obvious one. A path is little more than a habit that comes with knowledge of a place. It is a sort of ritual of familiarity. As a form, it is a form of contact with a known landscape. It is not destructive. It is the perfect adaptation, through experience and familiarity, of movement to place; it obeys the natural contours; such obstacles as it meets it goes around. A road, on the other hand, even the most primitive road, embodies a resistance against the landscape. Its reason is not simply the necessity for movement, but haste. Its wish is to avoid contact with the landscape; it seeks so far as possible to go over the country, rather than through it; its aspiration, as we see clearly in the example of our modern freeways, is to be a bridge; its tendency is to translate place into space in order to traverse it with the least effort. It is destructive, seeking to remove or destroy all obstacles in its way. The primitive road advanced by the destruction of the forest; modern roads advance by the destruction of topography.

Wendell Berry
Recollected Essays

E. ROBERT ROSS, *Guarded, Red Hill Valley,* ACRYLIC ON MASONITE, 51x61 CM, 1993.

Woe to those who add house to house

and join field to field

until everywhere belongs to them

and they are the sole inhabitants of the land.

Isaiah 5:8

Matthew Varey, *Scars and Open Wounds,* mixed media on wood construction, 183x183 cm, 1993.

Page 84

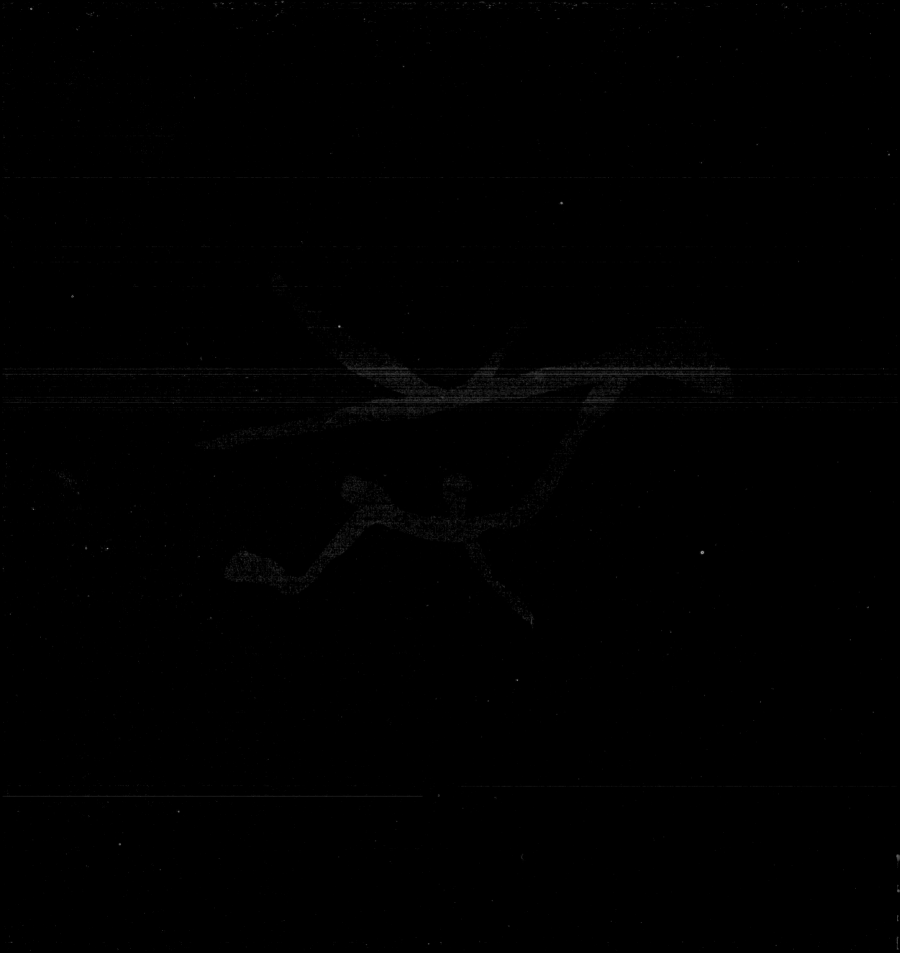

RENEWAL

WAY TO GO

West light flat on trees:

bird flying

deep out in blue glass:

uncertain wind

stirring the leaves: this is

the world we have:

take it

A.R. Ammons
Collected Poems 1951–1971

ROBERT CREIGHTON, *Two Trees,* MIXED MEDIA ON PAPER, 100x75 CM, 1993.

In approaching the land with an attitude of obligation, willing to observe courtesies difficult to articulate—perhaps only a gesture of the hands—one establishes a regard from which dignity can emerge. From that dignified relationship with the land, it is possible to imagine an extension of dignified relationships throughout one's life. Each relationship is formed of the same integrity, which initially makes the mind say: the things in the land fit together perfectly, even though they are always changing. I wish the order of my life to be arranged in the same way I find the light, the slight movement of the wind, the voice of a bird, the heading of a seed pod I see before me. This impeccable and indisputable integrity I want in myself....

An adult sensibility must find some way to include all the dark threads of life. A way to do this is to pay attention to what occurs in a land not touched by human schemes, where an original order prevails....

The European culture from which the ancestors of many of us came has yet to make this turn, I think. It has yet to understand the wisdom, preserved in North America, that lies in the richness and sanctity of a wild landscape, what it can mean in the unfolding of human life, the staying of a troubled human spirit.

Barry Lopez
Arctic Dreams

V. JANE GORDON, *Days and Nights in the Landscape (tree mounds)*, 500x127 CM, (Detail) *Before Dawn*, ACRYLIC ON CANVASETTE, EACH PANEL 30.5x40.7 CM, 1992.

Watching gardeners label their plants

I vow with all beings

to practice the old horticulture

and let the plants identify me.

Robert Aitken
The Dragon Who Never Sleeps:
Verse for Zen Buddhist Practice

Mary Toplack, *Sumac,* chalk pastel on rice paper, 40x55 cm, 1992.

Page 92

Western civilization has emphasized a distinctly
male way of relating to the world and has
organized itself around philosophical structures
that devalue the distinctly female approach to life.
For example, as the scientific and technological
revolution has picked up speed, we have seemed
to place a good deal more emphasis on technologies
that extend and magnify abilities—such as fight-
ing wars—historically associated more with males
than females. At the same time, new ways to
reduce our scandalously high rate of infant mor-
tality have received far less attention. Indeed, our
approach to technology itself has been shaped by
this same perspective: devices take precedent over
systems, ways to dominate nature receive more
attention than ways to work with nature.
Ultimately, part of the solution for the environmental crisis may well lie in our ability to achieve
a better balance between the sexes, leavening the
dominant male perspective with a healthier
respect for female ways of experiencing the world.

Al Gore
Earth in the Balance

Donna Ibing, *Eden Screen,* wood carved pine with acrylic, 183x76 cm, 1994.

Page 94

We must recognize the rights of each species to its habitat, to its migratory routes, to its place in the community. The bioregion is the domestic setting of the community just as the home is the domestic setting of the family. The community continues itself through successive generations precisely as a community. Both in terms of species and in terms of numbers, a certain balance must be maintained within the community. For humans to assume rights to occupy land by excluding other lifeforms from their needed habitat is to offend the community in its deepest structure. Further, it is even to declare a state of warfare, which humans cannot win since they themselves are ultimately dependent on those very life forms that they are destroying.

There is presently no other way for humans to educate themselves for survival and fulfillment than through the instruction available through the natural world.

Thomas Berry
The Dream of the Earth

BRENDA CARTER, *Dundas Valley Field Sketch,* WATERCOLOUR, 24x13 CM, 1991.

Sister bulrushes
stand and quietly
filter poisoned
water clean.

'Tis the gift to be simple
'Tis the gift to be free
'Tis the gift to come down
Where we ought to be
And when we are in
The place just right
Then we'll be in the Valley
Of love and delight

When true simplicity is here
To bow and to bend
We will not be ashamed
To turn, To turn
'Twill be our delight
Till by turning, turning
We come round right.

Shaker hymn

Barry Hodgson, *Red Hill Valley*, chalk pastel and tempera on paper, 50x55 cm, 1992.

Page 98

O Great Spirit, whose breath gives life to the world

and whose voice is heard in the soft breeze....

Make us wise so that we may understand what

you have taught us, help us learn the lessons you

have hidden in every leaf and rock...

Onondaga prayer

OWEN FORD, *Untitled,* OIL ON MASONITE, 60x50 CM, 1991.

THE HEAD OF THE LAKE

by Catherine Gibbon

PLACE & NAMES

The first European settlers approached the head of Lake Ontario by water. As they entered the waters of what had been called "Fond du Lac" by the French, the beauty of this distinctive landscape did not escape their notice. From the protected waters of the bay they viewed the gentle horizon of the escarpment heights as it enclosed a picturesque valley of forest and marsh. In deference to its pleasing appearance, the settlers called the bay Lake Geneva.

Over one hundred years before their arrival at the Head of the Lake, the towering primeval forest of pine, beech and maple supported a dense population of the Neutral nation. Described by the Recollet missionary D'Aillon as "taller, stronger and better proportioned" than their Huron allies, the Neutrals thrived in a rich environment that provided "an incredible number of stags...a great abundance of moose, elk, beaver, wildcats...a great quantity of wild geese, turkeys, cranes...excellent fish...and an abundance of squashes, beans and other vegetables." The native names for the head of the Lake reflect their sense of place. These names, *Ohronwagonh* or "in the valley," *Deonasadeo* or "where the sands form a bar" and *Macassa* or "place of sparkling waters," evoke the spirit of the landscape. They give a strong visual portrayal of the Head of the Lake as a sanctuary of beauty and protection.

The alteration of the landscape at the Head of the Lake, which continues to this day, was preceded by a change of names. In 1792, to the annoyance of some United Empire Loyalist residents, Lord Simcoe changed many of the names of the newly surveyed territory. Lake Geneva was now Burlington Bay. Of these new names, which mainly commemorated distinguished entrepreneurs and British aristocracy (such as Hamilton and Wentworth), Cootes Paradise is the most telling. It was named after British military officer and hunter Captain Thomas Coote, who viewed the abundant wildfowl of the marshes at the Head of the Lake with a predatory eye.

The Western incursion into the wilderness eventually led to the clearing of the primeval forest. Photographs of the Escarpment in the 1890s show barren slopes denuded of trees. Today, the ancestral remnants of the once pervasive Carolinian forest are fragmented into the three largest remaining green spaces in the region—the Beverly Swamp, the Dundas Valley and the Red Hill Valley. Large portions of these areas encompass the cliffs and valleys of the Niagara Escarpment, which runs like a green river through the city of Hamilton and is designated by UNESCO as a World Biosphere Reserve. As such, these local sanctuaries form an important link in this green corridor that extends over 700 kilometres across Southern Ontario, from Niagara to Tobermory. In addition to the habitats these areas provide for over 1,000 resident species, the Head of the Lake is strategically placed on migratory routes and is an important staging area for migrating birds.

The very qualities of the land that were once considered picturesque and formidable have restricted development in the region to its present precarious plateau. Today, although approximately 18% of the region is comprised of woodland, it is disproportionately distributed between east and west. Compared to the lush Dundas Valley, green space in the east end of the region is negligible, with the notable exception of the Red Hill Valley.

In 1993, the Hamilton Region was recognized internationally by the United Nations in its Local Agenda 21 Model Community Program for its efforts to restore and conserve its outstanding natural heritage. The importance and distinction of these remaining natural landscapes are often missed by some present-day residents and travellers to the Head of the Lake, many of whom enter the region on an expressway that offers a close view of the industrialized part of Burlington Bay. Yet, for the moment, the Head of the Lake is still uncommonly blessed.

As we approach the end of the 20th century, our choices become clearer. We must either abide by the laws of nature and learn to live as part of it or perish without it. We must re-evaluate our sense of place and reconsider the time when the Head of the Lake was called *Ohronwagonh*, a place of beauty and protection, offering both physical and spiritual renewal.

As dwellers on the land, in contact with the soil and the seasons, we can fashion a home, an identity, from what we find around us and from what we bring to it. The land has the power to shape us, to bring us together....
We might say of ourselves, "We are the people of the Bay, we are the city of waterfalls."

Farrell Boyce

SCRATCHBOARD ILLUSTRATIONS BY GORD PULLAR

BEVERLY SWAMP

1831

"It took Anderson four days to go from the farm of David Mulholland on the Eighth Concession to another farm on the tenth—a distance of 2 1/2 miles through pathless wilderness, having to cut logs, trees and brush."

1888 "There was once an immense quantity of choice pine timber in Beverly, but today it is scarce. People used to think there was no end to the cedars of Beverly, but the way it is going it will soon be a thing of the past. People who have it should use it with great care."

1950 "In Beverly Swamp on Lot 14, 8th Concession where there were some high elms, the fishing cranes had a large rookery. It was the only place in this area and is still in use by them every year, but fewer are coming back each year now."

These statements by residents of Beverly Township document the radical change in the landscape after 1800, when European settlers started to clear what they referred to as the "Great Cedar Swamp." Prior to the 19th century, the Beverly Swamp had remained in a natural state since its creation in the last Ice Age, when surface water was trapped by drumlins formed by deposits from retreating glaciers. After the glaciers disappeared, successive generations of native people populated the area, culminating in the Neutral Nation, who lived here at the time of the first European contact.

At the beginning of the 17th century the Beverly Swamp was part of what was known as *Terra Incognita* by the French, some of whom penetrated this area in their attempts to establish fur-trading networks with the natives. Although the French scout Etienne Brûlé encountered the Neutrals in 1615, the first written account of the area was recorded by the Récollet missionary Joseph de la Roche D'Aillon, who visited the Neutrals in 1626 in a failed attempt to convert them to Christianity. At that time, the palisaded villages and lands of the Neutrals supported the most densely populated Iroquoian settlement in northeastern North America. At least 13 of these settlements were

located near the Beverly Swamp, which provided habitat for the valuable fur-bearing beaver and muskrat.

Led by powerful warrior chief Souharrissen, the Neutrals flourished from their widespread trading contacts and rich environment. However, in a few short years after D'Aillon's visit, disease, famine and declining leadership completely undermined their social structure, leaving the Neutrals vulnerable to destructive trading conflicts with the Iroquois. By 1653, the Neutrals no longer existed as a cultural entity. Souharrissen was dead and the few remaining Neutrals were dispersed and absorbed by their native allies. Until European settlement began, the area was intermittently settled by peoples of the Algonkian and Seneca nations, many of whom established their villages on previous Neutral village sites. One of these villages, called *Tinawatawa*, was located a few miles from the present village of Westover, Ontario.

By 1850, much of Beverly Township was cleared. Snake and wolf hunting were diminishing in popularity as the clearing and draining of land destroyed natural habitats. Lumbering was in the final phase of its profitable but short history. Timber from the pine forests of Beverly was much sought after for the construction of masts on American sailing vessels. It was also used in the construction of buildings and roads. Beverly pioneers describe a plank road that stretched from Troy to Peters Corners as made of "pine planks about three inches thick and

as long as the road was wide which were laid on a bed of smaller logs."

Although much reduced from its original size, the remaining 5,000 acres of the Beverly Swamp provide an extremely important and environmentally sensitive habitat for a highly diverse and undisturbed biological community. Its resident species can be classified in several categories, which include northern species at their most southerly location in Ontario, rare and wetland species, and species dependent on large areas for survival.

Despite its ecological importance, the undisturbed interior of the Beverly Swamp remains the *Terra Incognita* of the present urban population that surrounds it.

Photo by Sylvester Maine. Reprinted by permission of Gladys Maine Grimyer-Grummet

DUNDAS VALLEY

The Dundas Valley is sheltered within the cliffs of the Niagara Escarpment and the marshes of Cootes Paradise. Its undulating and fertile terrain is crossed by numerous streams that cascade in waterfalls over the Escarpment. The largest of these is the Spencer Creek, which has its headwaters in the Beverly Swamp.

Four hundred million years ago, the Dundas Valley region was submerged under tropical seas. Successive layers of sediment from these seas formed the limestone bedrock that underlies the valley floor. Along the shores of this inland sea, the sedimentary rock was fractured and thin. As the ancient sea began to evaporate and recede, erosion carved a ridge along its former shores. This ridge was the first metamorphosis of the present Niagara Escarpment. As rivers crossed over the ridge, pre-glacial gorges, like the one that now lies deeply buried beneath the Dundas Valley, were formed.

Over 200 million years ago, the first wave of the Ice Age submerged the Dundas Valley under a kilometre of glacial ice. In the continuous advance and retreat of the ice, the valley was widened and scraped. Glacial deposits filled the valley, forming a series of hills that increase in height toward the western end of the valley. As the glaciers melted in retreat, the first land to emerge appeared as islands above the snow and ice. Finally released from the weight of ice some 180 million years later, the land began to rise to its present height.

Meanwhile, meltwaters from glaciers formed streams that collected into a huge river and flowed through the valley. Along the edges of these glacial rivers and streams, plants began to take root from seeds carried by wind and migrating birds. Muskox, mammoths and caribou wandered in these barren lands, grazing on lichens, mosses and cedars.

This original sparse vegetation eventually evolved into the climax forests of the Dundas Valley. As an elderly lumberman in 1916, W.D. Flatt of Dundas recalled the primeval forest that was still in existence in his childhood:

Right from the shores of Lake Ontario these counties were wooded with a primaeval forest that was inspiring in the extreme.... They presented to the pioneer a beauty, a grandeur, a solitude and mystery all so impressive.... The pine, the monarch of the forest, predominated, with oak, hickory, maple, beech, birch, spruce, cherry and butternut. The Creator was many generations in growing this wonderful forest crop. The grandeur and strength harmonized with the pioneer...wilderness in front of them, wilderness back of them, wilderness on all sides.

This rich forest environment was the setting of an important native portage route that had its origins in the previous 5,000 years of human settlement of the Valley. During the Neutral occupation of the region, this portage provided a vital link in a trading network between the more than 40 inland Neutral villages and distant parts of North America. The first Europeans in the area followed the trade route inland to other native trails, many of which are now roads in the region. Galinée, a Sulpician missionary

who accompanied La Salle into the Head of the Lake in 1669, described this route as follows:

We arrived at the end of Lake Ontario, where there is a fine large sandy bay at the bottom of which is an outlet to another little lake. This our guides made us enter about 1/2 a league, and unload our canoes...we pursued our journey sometimes in water up to mid-length, besides the inconvenience of the packs, which get caught on branches of trees.

OVENBIRD
Seiurus aurocapillus

Like the indigenous peoples, most of the early United Empire Loyalist settlers selected settlement sites above the Escarpment, which provided access to the fast moving streams and waterfalls required to power their mills. In addition to this, the Escarpment heights avoided the disturbing concentration of mosquitoes and rattlesnakes that flourished in the valley.

The flow of immigration and the development of the land continued unabated until 1850, when the Dundas Valley lost its prestigious title as the head of navigation on Lake Ontario to its economic competitor, Hamilton. In the decades that followed, nature began to reassert itself. The cleared, working landscape gave way as successions of field and forest ecosystems matured, filling in the open spaces with increasingly higher growth. Today, much of the Dundas Valley retains its historic characteristics, with precious large tracts of undisturbed forests where a few old-growth trees still remain. These forests and their connecting wooded corridors on the Niagara Escarpment provide habitat for many rare and endangered species that cannot tolerate human disturbance.

RED HILL VALLEY

When I was a child, I would hike out to Albion Falls every Good Friday with my friends. It was our annual rite of Spring, and judging from the number of kids to be found in the woods that day every year, it was here where most of us first experienced nature. You couldn't see any buildings. Tough kids seemed more mellow. We all seemed a little more equal. I felt stirrings of a sense of connection with things that I hadn't known before.

John Davies

The history and ecology of the Red Hill Valley reflect both the creative and destructive aspects of human interaction with natural environments. Its many legends and stories, customs and controversies, are a legacy of the connection between people and place.

This connection is renewed each year in a Good Friday ritual when hundreds of area residents flock to the valley for the hike described above by artist John Davies. Few ever forget the extraordinary experience of igniting the natural gas bubbles in the Red Hill Creek to cook their lunch on an open fire in the middle of the stream.

During the 19th century, numerous accounts circulated about strange lights, noises and ghosts that were experienced by frightened night travellers on the roads that skirted the head of the valley near Albion Falls under dense forest cover, and the northern end of the valley near Van Wagner's Marsh.

In 1929, the City of Hamilton purchased the Red Hill Valley for the future enjoyment of its citizens as "parkland that would be outstanding on this continent." In 1951, this "parkland" was proposed as an ideal site for an expressway. Since that time, its threatened destruction as a viable ecosystem and archaeological resource has polarized opinions in a controversy between environmental protection advocates and potential developers.

Human presence in the Red Hill Valley began at least 5,000 years ago when nomadic peoples of the pre-agricultural Iroquoian cultures fished and hunted the

Good Friday Hike at Albion Falls 1940. Reprinted by permission of the Dundas Historical Museum

valley's salmon and game. Their pathways along the banks of the Red Hill Creek connected with a wide-ranging network of trails, including what was later to be known as the Mohawk Trail. This land route (used by native peoples, including the Neutrals) connected native villages between Niagara and Brantford. From Niagara, it joined other trails in an easterly direction toward New York State's Hudson and Mohawk River valleys. In the late 1700s, the Six Nations and United Empire Loyalists used this route to flee harassment in the revolutionary United States. A few, like the Van Wagners, stopped in the Red Hill Valley. The first church, tavern and industries of the region were founded on the banks of the Red Hill Creek.

The natural history of the Red Hill Valley began with the formation of the Niagara Escarpment, of which it is part. At the end of the Ice Age, glacial runoff began to carve the course of the Red Hill Creek through the limestone and red shale bedrock that gave the valley its name. Originally draining into glacial Lake Iroquois, whose shore retreated to form Lake Ontario, the Red Hill Creek has followed its course for over 12,000 years. Before industrial development deprived much of Burlington Bay of its original marsh habitat, the Red Hill Creek emptied into what was one of the richest fish spawning areas in Lake Ontario, an area that also sustained an immense population of both migratory and resident birds.

Today, the Red Hill Valley is the only remaining large green space in the industrial east end of the city of Hamilton. Its varied topography creates a number of micro-climates that sustain many diverse species of life. At the intersection of two wooded corridors, it is one of the few woodland habitats in Southern Ontario that spans the distance between the Niagara Escarpment and Lake Ontario, and as such, it is depended upon by migrating birds who use it as a stopover point on their migration. Its wooded acres provide a valuable counterbalance to its present industrial surroundings, reducing air pollution and lowering summer temperatures.

Like all our natural lands, the Red Hill Valley preserves the record of its peoples and its timeless natural processes. It has remained in our midst as a living example of the care others have taken to preserve its natural integrity. Whatever evidence we choose to leave of our encounter with this striking landscape will demonstrate whether we are capable of showing a similar respect for the places we have inhabited.

It's open to us to try to do what is best not only for the wide world, but also for this small portion of the globe that embraces not only Cootes Paradise and my daughter's sky gripping silver maple, but also you and me.

Robert Clark Yates

ART FOR NATURE'S SAKE

by Regina Haggo

Knowing that art has the power to change the way people look at their surroundings, the artists associated with *On the Edge* have created work that celebrates the local natural environment and aims to ignite in the viewer a similar sense of celebration and respect. At the same time, their paintings, photographs and sculptures convey a warning: the green space that hugs the sprawling urban centre is disappearing.

On the one hand, the art of *On the Edge* fits within a regionalist idiom. Regionalism encourages an artist to identify with the community she or he inhabits. It encourages artists to make art about the area they live in and for people they live with. The works have been inspired by specific local sites: Beverly Swamp, Dundas Valley and Red Hill Valley. On the other hand, the art goes beyond the regional, since its message is universal; the natural environment is worth preserving worldwide, not just locally.

In terms of genre, most of these works find their place in the Western landscape tradition, which has its roots in art created 2,000 years ago in the Roman Empire. To urbanites in noisy, crowded cities such as Rome, landscape paintings and reliefs offered a kind of spiritual retreat. By the second century, the artistic symbol of paradise was a lush, green landscape. At the same time, another tradition was developing, one in which nature stood between human beings and civilization, represented by cities, roads and bridges. The destruction of forests symbolized progress. It was not until the 19th century that some people began to view the expansion of civilization—in the shape of railways, for example—as a threat to the natural environment.

Landscape painting played a leading role in the Romantic movement that began in the late 18th century. In Romantic works, nature often reflected the artist's state of mind, and could be portrayed as threatening, terrifying, unpredictable or calming. Landscape became such a noble genre that some critics declared that female artists were not competent physically and morally to undertake it. In Canada, the popularity of the Group of Seven has helped to lift landscape painting to a position above other genres.

Unlike many Canadian landscape artists, the artists of *On the Edge* have concentrated on responding to the natural world close to home. In Catherine Gibbon's *Thunderbolt*, a dark, volatile sky dominates a calmer but brighter section of land and trees. The swirling activity in the upper zone threatens to tear the whole landscape apart. E. Robert Ross's *Cootes Paradise* also works with layers, starting with rippling water at the bottom and making its way up to a dramatic cloud-filled sky. His paintings are sharper and less abstract than Gibbon's. Robert Clark Yates adopts an aerial perspective in *Red Hill Valley*, creating a painting that is map-like and pictographic. Linda Hankin's *By the Barn Overlooking the Valley* is full of fluid forms emphasizing the variety of trees in the Dundas Valley. In *Red Hill Valley*, Barry Hodgson mixes simple shapes and bright colours that record his reactions to the richness of nature around him. Barbara Guy Long's *Dancing on the Edge* is landscape interpreted as rhythmical riot of colour forming an abstracted and highly energetic composition.

Works by Patricia Kozowyk, John Davies and Elizabeth Halliwell illustrate three approaches to painting trees, particularly with respect to the viewer's relationship to the setting. All three put the viewer in a forest. In Kozowyk's *Winter Woods*, a blanket of snow covers the bases of the trunks, while the treetops extend beyond the picture space. The trunks, painted in a hard-edged style, are consistently straight and vertical. The trees do not block the viewer's way into the work, but the absence of human footprints in the snow suggests that entering would be intrusive. By contrast, John Davies's *Escarpment Forest* relies less on verticals. His black-outlined trees bend, twist, grow and fall on a brightly coloured forest floor. Diagonal trunks in the midground form a kind of barrier, hindering our entry into the picture. Elizabeth Halliwell's *Trees Please* is similar in subject and viewpoint, but her style is less linear than that of Kozowyk or Davies, and her tightly packed trees keep the viewer at a respectful distance.

Though most of the *On the Edge* work is nonfigural, the human figure does appear, or is hinted at, with powerful results. In Jim Riley's *Under Pressure*, a man with a landscape on his torso holds a heavy chain hanging from his neck. Yates's *Red Hill Valley* contains footprints of two generations, the artist's and his daughter's. Other paintings point to the presence of people in more subtle ways. Matthew Varey's *Scars and Open Wounds* presents an aerial view of a vividly coloured landscape abused by humans. Gordon Pullar's *Buttermilk Falls* is a close-up view of nature despoiled by its inhabitants—littered with garbage and graffiti. This landscape is alarming because it is not imaginary. Tracey Bowen's *Swamp Angel* refers to the figure in quite a different way. Her totem-like sculpture is anthropomorphic but appears to represent a spirit of the forest or some other part of nature.

The works discussed here demonstrate some of the interpretive possibilities open to both viewer and artist. Since the artists are environmental activists, the pieces they create are not only aesthetic objects; they have a purpose that is social, political, ethical. The viewer is meant to think about the environment's precarious position—and to do something to help save it.

SPONSORING ORGANIZATIONS

THE CONSERVER SOCIETY

A lot has changed in our perception of the world around us since the publication of Rachel Carson's *Silent Spring* in the late 1960s. The more we learn about the earth, the more we realize how out of sync we have become with her ways. Fundamental changes to attitudes and lifestyle are required of all of us.

Environmental activists are always seeking new cultural and educational tools to reach people with their message. Art is a powerful tool that can help shape our perceptions of Mother Earth. By bringing artists and environmentalists together, we can help save the planet for the benefit of future generations of all life forms.

The Conserver Society of Hamilton and District is proud to be a co-sponsor of the ON THE EDGE, a project that has broken new ground in our efforts to develop a new conserver lifestyle that is ecologically sustainable. The project has enriched the lives of all its participants, with new ideas, new experiences and new contacts.

The Conserver Society is a network of individuals, chapters and affiliated organizations dedicated to building a better future in which humans can live in harmony with nature. Join us, and play a part. Through our newsletter and public events, you can learn how to live the conserver way. For information, write to us c/o 255 West Ave. N., Hamilton, ON L8L 5C8 or call us at (905) 522-5779.

Peter Hutton, Chair, Conserver Society

THE CARNEGIE GALLERY

The Carnegie Gallery is located in the heart of the Dundas Valley in the town of Dundas. As a active participant in the promotion of the visual arts in the community, this non-profit gallery has sponsored a number of projects that have contributed to the vitality of the cultural life within the region. None of these has involved the imagination and active participation of the community to the same extent as ON THE EDGE.

It was only natural that the ON THE EDGE project developed under the co-sponsorship of the Carnegie Gallery. Over the past several years many of our exhibits have explored the theme of landscape. Deep concerns about the environmental crisis that threatens the Dundas Valley and our region have surfaced time and time again, in art and artists' statements.

ON THE EDGE reflects the concerns and hopes that artists have for their local environment. It brings together different interest groups and diverse forms of expression in an effort to make us look at our surrounding natural environments in a new way. As such, it is a superb example of the creative forces that artists can manifest in our community.

The Carnegie Gallery is very proud of its affiliation with ON THE EDGE. We believe that the gallery provided a focus and channel—sometimes even an outlet—for the ideas behind the project. But it is the individual artists themselves who deserve credit for the conviction of their ideas and the sincerity of their efforts to create a sustainable future.

Jane Nahirny Zatylny
Carnegie Gallery
10 King Street West
Dundas, ON
L9H 1T7
(905) 627-4265

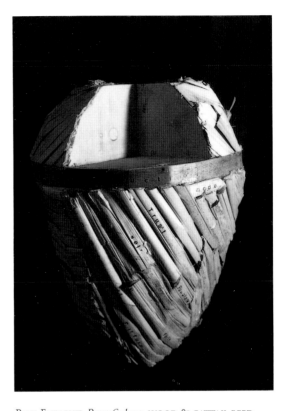

PAUL ENRIGHT, *Proto Sphere,* WOOD & CATTAIL REED, 45x23x22 CM., 1992.

ACKNOWLEDGEMENTS

On the Edge: Artistic Visions of a Shrinking Landscape represents the culmination of the ON THE EDGE Art/Environment project. This project, sponsored by the Carnegie Gallery of Dundas and the Conserver Society of Hamilton, brought together artists, writers, musicians, environmentalists, students, and members of the community in an effort to focus attention on the value of the natural environments of the Hamilton–Wentworth region. The enthusiastic support and participation in the camps, exhibitions, and celebrations of this project testify to the care and concern of the community at the Head of the Lake for their near natural environments.

We wish to thank all those individuals and organizations, especially

Richard Allen

Blackberry Hill Farm

The Broadway Cinema

Gord & Pat Cameron

The Carnegie Gallery

The Conserver Society

Bert Dorpmans of McMaster Framing

Bruce Duncan

The Environmental Research Trust

The Hamilton and Region Conservation Authority

Elizabeth Halliwell

Peter Hutton

Jose Crespo

Shannon Kyles and the mural painters from the Architecture Club of Mohawk College

Laidlaw Waste Systems

Doug Larson

Stewart Leslie

Don McLean

Jane Nahirny Zatylny

Bill Noble

Nancy McKibbin

The Ministry of Culture, Tourism, and Recreation

Graham Petrie

Sue Powell

Gord Pullar

Pushpa & Chethan Sathya

Margaret Schooley

Sheraine Seepaul

David Seldon

Oliver Slupecki

Ulf Stahmer

Beth Stormont

John Terpstra

The World Wildlife Fund

all of the ON THE EDGE artists & the ON THE EDGE committee members:

Farrell Boyce

Catherine Gibbon

Regina & Doug Haggo

Barry Hodgson

Patricia Kozowyk

Mike Perozak

Adele Taylor-Pick & Walter Pick

Robert Ross

We gratefully acknowledge financial support for this publication from

THE BERTRAM FOUNDATION

CANADA TRUST

THE ENVIRONMENTAL RESEARCH TRUST

THE HAMILTON COMMUNITY FOUNDATION

THE MCBRIDE FOUNDATION

ONTARIO ARTS COUNCIL

& THE ONTARIO HERITAGE FOUNDATION THROUGH THE NIAGARA ESCARPMENT PROGRAM.

This book is dedicated to the people of the ancient forests, streams and skies of the Head of the Lake.

BIBLIOGRAPHY

WORKS CITED

Ammons, A.R. *Collected Poems 1951-1971*. New York: W.W. Norton and Company, 1972.

Anderson, Lorraine (ed.). *Sisters of the Earth*. Toronto: Random House, 1991.

Atwood, Margaret. *The Journals of Susanna Moodie*. Toronto: Oxford University Press, 1970.

Berry, Thomas. *The Dream of the Earth*. San Francisco: Sierra Club Books, 1990.

Berry, Wendell. *Collected Poems 1957-1982*. San Francisco: North Point Press, 1984.

———. *Recollected Essays 1965-1980*. San Francisco: North Point Press, 1981.

Beverly Municipality (ed.) *Pioneers of Beverly*. 1967.

Boyce, Farrell. "A Song for My Home." *Hamilton Spectator*, April 17, 1993.

Butala, Sharon. *The Perfection of the Morning: An Apprenticeship in Nature*. Toronto: HarperCollins Publishers Ltd., 1994.

Carr, Emily. *Hundreds and Thousands: The Journals of an Artist*. Toronto: Irwin Publishing Inc., 1986.

Coyne. "Father Galinée's Narrative," Ontario Historical Society Papers and Records. Vol. 4, 1903.

Flatt, W.D. *The Trail of Love: An Appreciation of Canadian Pioneers and Pioneer Life*. Toronto: Willian Briggs, 1916.

Gore, Al. *Earth in the Balance: Ecology and the Human Spirit*. New York: Plume, 1993.

Horwood, Harold. *Dancing on the Shore: A Celebration of Life at Annapolis Basin*. Toronto: McClelland and Stewart, 1987.

Inksetter, Helen. "Pioneer Days in Beverly" in Papers and Records of the Wentworth Historical Society, Vol. 7, 1916.

Johnson, Pauline. *Flint and Feather*. Toronto: Musson Book Co. Ltd., 1931.

Johnston, Basil. *Ojibway Heritage: The ceremonies, rituals, songs, dances, prayers, and legends of the Ojibway*. Toronto: McClelland and Stewart Inc., 1990.

Johnston C.M. *The Head of the Lake; A History of Wentworth County*. Hamilton: Robert and Duncan Co., 1967.

Kappel-Smith, Diana. *Wintering*. Boston: Little, Brown and Company Ltd., 1984.

Keough, Pat and Rosemarie. *The Niagara Escarpment*. Don Mills: Stoddart Publishing Co., 1990.

Leopold, Aldo. *A Sand County Almanac*. San Francisco: Sierra Club, 1970.

Lopez, Barry. *Crossing Open Ground*. New York: Charles Scribner's Sons, 1988.

———. *Arctic Dreams: Imagination and Desire in a Northern Landscape*. New York: Charles Scribner's Sons, 1986.

McKibben, Bill. *The End of Nature*. New York: Doubleday, 1990.

Noble, Wm.C. "Historic Neutral Iroquois Settlement Patterns." *Canadian Journal of Archaeology* Vol. 8 (no. 1), 1984.

Pack, Robert. "The Trees will Die." *Georgia Review,* Summer 1994.

Rexroth, Kenneth. *One Hundred Poems from the Japanese*. New York: New Directions Books, 1964.

———. *Love and the Turning Year: One Hundred More Poems from the Chinese*. New York: New Directions Books, 1970.

Roberts, Elizabeth (ed.). *Earth Prayers*. New York: HarperCollins Publisher, 1991.

Slipperjack, Ruby. "Interview." *Contemporary Challenges: Conversations with Canadian Native Writers*. Hartmut Lutz (ed). Saskatoon: Fifth House Publishers, 1991.

Stegner, Wallace. *The Sound of Mountain Water*. Lincoln: University of Nebraska Press, 1985.

Terpstra, John. *Naked Trees*. Windsor, Ontario: Netherlandic Press, 1990.

Thwaites, R.G. (ed.) *The Jesuit Relations and Allied Documents,* Vol. 21. Cleveland: Burrows, 1901.

Trask, Haunani-Kay Trask. *Global Visions*. Montreal: Black Rose Books Ltd., 1993.

Turner, J.E. "The History of Albion Falls." Unpublished manuscript, Hamilton Public Library, 1946.

Weaver, John C. *Hamilton; An Illustrated History.* Toronto: James Lorimer and Co., 1982.

Yates, Robert Clark. "Where We Live." Copyright Robert Clark Yates.

COPYRIGHT ACKNOWLEDGEMENTS